God's

Word

Gives...

Karen L. Howard

Table of Contents

**All quoted scripture is taken from the Old Testament of the Holy Bible, King James Version.

"... man doth not live by bread only, but by every word that proceedeth out of the mouth of the LORD doth man live."
Deuteronomy 8:3

"And I will give them a heart to know me, that I am the LORD: and they shall be my people, and I will be their God: for they shall return unto me with their whole heart." Jeremiah 24:7

"I delight to do thy will, O my God: yea, thy law is within my heart." Psalms 40:8

"Behold, I am the LORD, the God of all flesh: is there any thing too hard for me?"
Jeremiah 32:27

God's Word Gives Blessings...

"The LORD bless thee, and keep thee: The LORD make his face shine upon thee, and be gracious unto thee: The LORD lift up his countenance upon thee, and give thee peace. And they shall put my name upon their children... and I will bless them."
Numbers 6:24-27

"His name shall endure for ever: his name shall be continued as long as the sun: and men shall be blessed in him: all nations shall call him blessed." Psalms 72:17

"For I will pour water upon him that is thirsty, and floods upon the dry ground: I will pour my spirit upon thy seed, and my blessing upon thine offspring". Isaiah 44:3

"Blessed is the man whose strength is in thee; in whose heart are the ways of them." Psalms 84:5

"Blessed is the man that walketh not in the counsel of the ungodly, nor standeth in the way of sinners, nor sitteth in the seat of the scornful. But his delight is in the law of the LORD; and in his law doth he meditate day and night." Psalms 1:1-2

"And there ye shall eat before the LORD your God, and ye shall rejoice in all that ye put your hand unto, ye and your households, wherein the LORD thy God hath blessed thee." Deuteronomy 12:7

"They shall not labour in vain, nor bring forth for trouble; for they are the seed of the blessed of the LORD, and their offspring with them." Isaiah 65:23

"Blessed is he whose transgression is forgiven, whose sin is covered." Psalms 32:1

"The curse of the LORD is in the house of the wicked: but he blesseth the habitation of the just." Proverbs 3:33

"God be merciful unto us, and bless us; and cause his face to shine upon us; That thy way may be known upon earth, thy saving health among all nations." Psalms 67:1

"And therefore will the LORD wait, that he may be gracious unto you, and therefore will he be exalted, that he may have mercy upon you: for the LORD is a God of judgment: blessed are all they that wait for him." Isaiah 30:18

"The just man walketh in his integrity: his children are blessed after him."
Proverbs 20:7

"Blessed is every one that feareth the LORD; that walketh in his ways."
Psalms 128:1

"Blessed is the man that doeth this, and the son of man that layeth hold on it; that keepeth the sabbath from polluting it, and keepeth his hand from doing any evil."
Isaiah 56:2

"He that hath clean hands, and a pure heart; who hath not lifted up his soul unto vanity, nor sworn deceitfully. He shall receive the blessing from the LORD, and righteousness from the God of his salvation." Psalms 24:4-5

"O taste and see that the LORD is good: blessed is the man that trusteth in him."
Psalms 34:8

"Now therefore hearken unto me, O ye children: for blessed are they that keep my ways." Proverbs 8:32

"Blessed is he that considereth the poor: the LORD will deliver him in time of trouble. The LORD will preserve him, and keep him alive; and he shall be blessed upon the earth: and thou wilt not deliver him unto the will of his enemies." Psalms 41:1-2

"Blessed is the man unto whom the LORD imputeth not iniquity, and in whose spirit there is no guile." Psalms 32:2

"And their seed shall be known among the Gentiles, and their offspring among the people: all that see them shall acknowledge them, that they are the seed which the LORD hath blessed." Isaiah 61:9

"For thou, LORD, wilt bless the righteous; with favour wilt thou compass him as with a shield." Psalms 5:12

"Ye are blessed of the LORD which made heaven and earth. The heaven, even the heavens, are the LORD'S: but the earth hath he given to the children of men." Psalms 115:15

"And I will bless them that bless thee, and curse him that curseth thee: and in thee shall all families of the earth be blessed." Genesis 12:3

"Bring ye all the tithes into the storehouse, that there may be meat in mine house, and prove me now herewith, saith the LORD of hosts, if I will not open you the windows of heaven, and pour you out a blessing, that there shall not be room enough to receive it." Malachi 3:10

God's Word Gives Salvation...

"Behold, God is my salvation; I will trust, and not be afraid: for the LORD JEHOVAH is my strength and my song; he also is become my salvation." Isaiah 12:2

"Truly my soul waiteth upon God: from him cometh my salvation. He only is my rock and my salvation; he is my defence; I shall not be greatly moved." Psalms 62:1-2

"I am the LORD thy God... and thou shalt know no god but me: for there is no saviour beside me." Hosea 13:4

"Lead me in thy truth, and teach me: for thou art the God of my salvation; on thee do I wait all the day." Psalms 25:5

11

"Forsake me not, O LORD: O my God, be not far from me. Make haste to help me, O Lord my salvation." Psalms 38:21-22

"For I am the LORD thy God, the Holy One of Israel, thy Saviour". Isaiah 43:3

"And wisdom and knowledge shall be the stability of thy times, and strength of salvation: the fear of the LORD is his treasure." Isaiah 33:6

"Thus saith the LORD, Keep ye judgment, and do justice: for my salvation is near to come, and my righteousness to be revealed." Isaiah 56:1

"The LORD is my strength and song, and is become my salvation." Psalms 118:14

"Help us, O God of our salvation, for the glory of thy name: and deliver us, and purge away our sins, for thy name's sake."
Psalms 79:9

"O LORD, be gracious unto us; we have waited for thee: be thou their arm every morning, our salvation also in the time of trouble." Isaiah 33:2

"And it shall be said in that day, Lo, this is our God; we have waited for him, and he will save us: this is the LORD; we have waited for him, we will be glad and rejoice in his salvation." Isaiah 25:9

"Whoso offereth praise glorifieth me: and to him that ordereth his conversation aright will I shew the salvation of God."
Psalms 50:23

"Save us, O God of our salvation, and gather us together, and deliver us from the heathen, that we may give thanks to thy holy name, and glory in thy praise."
1 Chronicles 16:35

"Therefore I will look unto the LORD; I will wait for the God of my salvation: my God will hear me." Micah 7:7

"... there is no God else beside me; a just God and a Saviour; there is none beside me. Look unto me, and be ye saved, all the ends of the earth: for I am God, and there is none else." Isaiah 45:21-22

"Shew us thy mercy, O LORD, and grant us thy salvation. I will hear what God the LORD will speak: for he will speak peace unto his people, and to his saints: but let them not turn again to folly." Psalms 85:7-8

"Thou art my father, my God, and the rock of my salvation." Psalms 89:26

"But the salvation of the righteous is of the LORD: he is their strength in the time of trouble. And the LORD shall help them, and deliver them: he shall deliver them from the wicked, and save them, because they trust in him." Psalms 37:39-40

"The God of my rock; in him will I trust: he is my shield, and the horn of my salvation, my high tower, and my refuge, my saviour; thou savest me from violence. I will call on the LORD, who is worthy to be praised: so shall I be saved from mine enemies."
2 Samuel 22:3-4

"Preserve my soul; for I am holy: O thou my God, save thy servant that trusteth in thee." Psalms 86:2

"Let thy mercies come also unto me, O LORD, even thy salvation, according to thy word." Psalms 119:41

"... they cry unto the LORD in their trouble, and he bringeth them out of their distresses." Psalms 107:28

"I have blotted out, as a thick cloud, thy transgressions, and, as a cloud, thy sins: return unto me; for I have redeemed thee." Isaiah 44:22

"He only is my rock and my salvation: he is my defence; I shall not be moved. In God is my salvation and my glory: the rock of my strength, and my refuge, is in God. Trust in him at all times; ye people, pour out your heart before him: God is a refuge for us." Psalms 62:6-7

"The LORD liveth; and blessed be my rock; and let the God of my salvation be exalted." Psalms 18:46

"For the LORD taketh pleasure in his people: he will beautify the meek with salvation." Psalms 149:4

"Let all those that seek thee rejoice and be glad in thee: and let such as love thy salvation say continually, Let God be magnified. But I am poor and needy: make haste unto me, O God: thou art my help and my deliverer; O LORD, make no tarrying." Psalms 70:4-5

"But I have trusted in thy mercy; my heart shall rejoice in thy salvation." Psalms 13:5

God's Word Gives Joy...

"Sing unto God, sing praises to his name: extol him that rideth upon the heavens by his name YAH, and rejoice before him."
Psalms 68:4

"Yet I will rejoice in the LORD, I will joy in the God of my salvation." Habakkuk 3:18

"But let all those that put their trust in thee rejoice: let them ever shout for joy, because thou defendest them: let them also that love thy name be joyful in thee."
Psalms 5:11

"Be glad in the LORD, and rejoice, ye righteous: and shout for joy, all ye that are upright in heart." Psalms 32:11

"The LORD thy God in the midst of thee is mighty; he will save, he will rejoice over thee with joy; he will rest in his love, he will joy over thee with singing."
Zephaniah 3:17

"They that sow in tears shall reap in joy."
Psalms 126:5

"Deceit is in the heart of them that imagine evil: but to the counsellors of peace is joy." Proverbs 12:20

"A merry heart doeth good like a medicine: but a broken spirit drieth the bones."
Proverbs 17:22

"Thou wilt shew me the path of life: in thy presence is fulness of joy; at thy right hand there are pleasures for evermore."
Psalms 16:11

"For his anger endureth but a moment; in his favour is life: weeping may endure for a night, but joy cometh in the morning." Psalms 30:5

"For ye shall go out with joy, and be led forth with peace: the mountains and the hills shall break forth before you into singing, and all the trees of the field shall clap their hands." Isaiah 55:12

"And my soul shall be joyful in the LORD: it shall rejoice in his salvation." Psalms 35:9

"O come, let us sing unto the LORD: let us make a joyful noise to the rock of our salvation. Let us come before his presence with thanksgiving, and make a joyful noise unto him with psalms." Psalms 95:1-2

"Even them will I bring to my holy mountain, and make them joyful in my house of prayer... for mine house shall be called a house of prayer for all people."
Isaiah 56:7

"Blessed is the people that know the joyful sound: they shall walk, O LORD, in the light of thy countenance. In thy name shall they rejoice all the day: and in thy righteousness shall they be exalted." Psalms 89:15

"Make a joyful noise unto the LORD, all the earth: make a loud noise, and rejoice, and sing praise." Psalms 98:4

"Rejoice in the LORD, O ye righteous: for praise is comely for the upright."
Psalms 33:1

"My meditation of him shall be sweet: I will be glad in the LORD." Psalms 104:34

"In thy name shall they rejoice all the day: and in thy righteousness shall they be exalted. For thou art the glory of their strength: and in thy favour our horn shall be exalted." Psalms 89:16

"I will greatly rejoice in the LORD, my soul shall be joyful in my God; for he hath clothed me with the garments of salvation, he hath covered me with the robe of righteousness, as a bridegroom decketh himself with ornaments, and as a bride adorneth herself with her jewels." Isaiah 61:10

"The light of the righteous rejoiceth: but the lamp of the wicked shall be put out." Proverbs 13:9

"Thy words were found, and I did eat them; and thy word was unto me the joy and rejoicing of mine heart: for I am called by thy name, O LORD God of hosts."
Jeremiah 15:16

"But let the righteous be glad; let them rejoice before God: yea, let them exceedingly rejoice." Psalms 68:3

"The statutes of the LORD are right, rejoicing the heart: the commandment of the LORD is pure, enlightening the eyes."
Psalms 19:8

"Let the heavens rejoice, and let the earth be glad; let the sea roar, and the fulness thereof. Let the field be joyful, and all that is therein: then shall all the trees of the wood rejoice before the LORD".
Psalms 96:11-12

God's Word Gives Guidance...

"For thou art my rock and my fortress; therefore for thy name's sake lead me, and guide me." Psalms 31:3

"They shall not hunger nor thirst; neither shall the heat nor sun smite them: for he that hath mercy on them shall lead them, even by the springs of water shall he guide them." Isaiah 49:10

"And the LORD shall guide thee continually, and satisfy thy soul in drought, and make fat thy bones: and thou shalt be like a watered garden, and like a spring of water, whose waters fail not." Isaiah 58:11

"A man's heart deviseth his way: but the LORD directeth his steps." Proverbs 16:9

"The LORD is my shepherd; I shall not want. He maketh me to lie down in green pastures: he leadeth me beside the still waters. He restoreth my soul: he leadeth me in the paths of righteousness for his name's sake. Yea, though I walk through the valley of the shadow of death, I will fear no evil: for thou art with me; thy rod and thy staff they comfort me. Thou preparest a table before me in the presence of mine enemies: thou anointest my head with oil; my cup runneth over. Surely goodness and mercy shall follow me all the days of my life: and I will dwell in the house of the LORD for ever."
Psalms 23:1-6

"I cannot go beyond the commandment of the LORD, to do either good or bad of mine own mind; but what the LORD saith, that will I speak?" Numbers 24:13

"For this God is our God for ever and ever: he will be our guide even unto death."
Psalms 48:14

"So the LORD alone did lead him, and there was no strange god with him."
Deuteronomy 32:12

"Teach me to do thy will; for thou art my God: thy spirit is good; lead me into the land of uprightness." Psalms 143:10

"Lead me, O LORD, in thy righteousness because of mine enemies; make thy way straight before my face." Psalms 5:8

"The steps of a good man are ordered by the LORD: and he delighteth in his way. Though he fall, he shall not be utterly cast down: for the LORD upholdeth him with his hand." Psalms 37:23

"And thine ears shall hear a word behind thee, saying, This is the way, walk ye in it, when ye turn to the right hand, and when ye turn to the left." Isaiah 30:21

"Shew me thy ways, O LORD; teach me thy paths. Lead me in thy truth, and teach me…". Psalms 25:4

"Train up a child in the way he should go: and when he is old, he will not depart from it." Proverbs 22:6

"And these words, which I command thee this day, shall be in thine heart: And thou shalt teach them diligently unto thy children, and shalt talk of them when thou sittest in thine house, and when thou walkest by the way, and when thou liest down, and when thou risest up."
Deuteronomy 6:6-7

"He shall feed his flock like a shepherd: he shall gather the lambs with his arm, and carry them in his bosom, and shall gently lead those that are with young."
Isaiah 40:11

"And the LORD went before them by day in a pillar of a cloud, to lead them the way; and by night in a pillar of fire, to give them light; to go by day and night". Exodus 13:21

"And I will bring the blind by a way that they knew not; I will lead them in paths that they have not known: I will make darkness light before them, and crooked things straight. These things will I do unto them, and not forsake them." Isaiah 42:16

"The law of his God is in his heart; none of his steps shall slide." Psalms 37:31

"I will instruct thee and teach thee in the way which thou shalt go: I will guide thee with mine eye." Psalms 32:8

"The meek will he guide in judgment: and the meek will he teach his way. All the paths of the LORD are mercy and truth unto such as keep his covenant and his testimonies." Psalms 25:9-10

"Out of heaven he made thee to hear his voice, that he might instruct thee".
Deuteronomy 4:36

"Thus saith the LORD, thy Redeemer, the Holy One of Israel; I am the LORD thy God which teacheth thee to profit, which leadeth thee by the way that thou shouldest go." Isaiah 48:17

"I waited patiently for the LORD; and he inclined unto me, and heard my cry. He brought me up also out of a horrible pit, out of the miry clay, and set my feet upon a rock, and established my goings. And he hath put a new song in my mouth, even praise unto our God: many shall see it, and fear, and shall trust in the LORD."
Psalms 40:1-3

"Trust in the LORD with all thine heart; and lean not unto thine own understanding. In all thy ways acknowledge him, and he shall direct thy paths. Be not wise in thine own eyes: fear the LORD, and depart from evil."
Proverbs 3:5-7

"And the LORD, he it is that doth go before thee; he will be with thee, he will not fail thee, neither forsake thee: fear not, neither be dismayed." Deuteronomy 31:8

God's Word Gives Reassurance...

"When thou art in tribulation, and all these things are come upon thee, even in the latter days, if thou turn to the LORD thy God, and shalt be obedient unto his voice; For the LORD thy God is a merciful God; he will not forsake thee, neither destroy thee...". Deuteronomy 4:30-31

"The LORD is with you, while ye be with him; and if ye seek him, he will be found of you; but if ye forsake him, he will forsake you." 2 Chronicles 15:2

"Acquaint now thyself with him, and be at peace: thereby good shall come unto thee." Job 22:21

"But the meek shall inherit the earth; and shall delight themselves in the abundance of peace." Psalms 37:11

"Cast thy burden upon the LORD, and he shall sustain thee: he shall never suffer the righteous to be moved." Psalms 55:22

"The LORD shall preserve thee from all evil: he shall preserve thy soul. The LORD shall preserve thy going out and thy coming in from this time forth, and even for evermore." Psalms 121:7-8

"When thou passest through the waters, I will be with thee; and through the rivers, they shall not overflow thee: when thou walkest through the fire, thou shalt not be burned; neither shall the flame kindle upon thee." Isaiah 43:2

"If thou shalt hearken unto the voice of the LORD thy God, to keep his commandments and his statutes which are written in this book of the law, and if thou turn unto the LORD thy God with all thine heart, and with all thy soul. For this commandment which I command thee this day, it is not hidden from thee, neither is it far off. It is not in heaven, that thou shouldest say, Who shall go up for us to heaven, and bring it unto us, that we may hear it, and do it? Neither is it beyond the sea, that thou shouldest say, Who shall go over the sea for us, and bring it unto us, that we may hear it, and do it? But the word is very nigh unto thee, in thy mouth, and in thy heart, that thou mayest do it... In that I command thee this day to love the LORD thy God, to walk in his ways... that thou mayest live and multiply: and the LORD thy God shall bless thee".

Deuteronomy 30:10-16

"When my father and my mother forsake me, then the LORD will take me up."
Psalms 27:10

"I will lift up mine eyes unto the hills, from whence cometh my help. My help cometh from the LORD, which made heaven and earth. He will not suffer thy foot to be moved: he that keepeth thee will not slumber." Psalms 121:1-3

"He sent redemption unto his people: he hath commanded his covenant for ever: holy and reverend is his name."
Psalms 111:9

"Then said he unto me, Fear not... for from the first day that thou didst set thine heart to understand, and to chasten thyself before thy God, thy words were heard...".
Daniel 10:12

"For the LORD will not forsake his people for his great name's sake: because it hath pleased the LORD to make you his people." 1 Samuel 12:22

"I am sought of them that asked not for me; I am found of them that sought me not: I said, Behold me, behold me, unto a nation that was not called by my name." Isaiah 65:1

"Let the wicked forsake his way, and the unrighteous man his thoughts: and let him return unto the LORD, and he will have mercy upon him; and to our God, for he will abundantly pardon." Isaiah 55:7

"For the righteous LORD loveth righteousness; his countenance doth behold the upright." Psalms 11:7

"When the poor and needy seek water, and there is none, and their tongue faileth for thirst, I the LORD will hear them, I the God of Israel will not forsake them."
Isaiah 41:17

"But if from thence thou shalt seek the LORD thy God, thou shalt find him, if thou seek him with all thy heart and with all thy soul." Deuteronomy 4:29

"Keep thy heart with all diligence; for out of it are the issues of life." Proverbs 4:23

"For he shall give his angels charge over thee, to keep thee in all thy ways. They shall bear thee up in their hands, lest thou dash thy foot against a stone."
Psalms 91:11-12

God's Word Gives Praise...

"Stand up and bless the LORD your God for ever and ever: and blessed be thy glorious name, which is exalted above all blessing and praise. Thou, even thou, art LORD alone; thou hast made heaven, the heaven of heavens, with all their host, the earth, and all things that are therein, the seas, and all that is therein, and thou preservest them all; and the host of heaven worshippeth thee." Nehemiah 9:5-6

"I will praise the LORD according to his righteousness: and will sing praise to the name of the LORD most high." Psalms 7:17

"Let my mouth be filled with thy praise and with thy honour all the day." Psalms 71:8

"O LORD our Lord, how excellent is thy name in all the earth! who hast set thy glory above the heavens." Psalms 8:1

"Make a joyful noise unto the LORD, all ye lands. Serve the LORD with gladness: come before his presence with singing. Know ye that the LORD he is God: it is he that hath made us, and not we ourselves; we are his people, and the sheep of his pasture. Enter into his gates with thanksgiving, and into his courts with praise: be thankful unto him, and bless his name. For the LORD is good; his mercy is everlasting; and his truth endureth to all generations."
Psalms 100:1-5

"Be thou exalted, O God, above the heavens; let thy glory be above all the earth." Psalms 57:5

"Because thy lovingkindness is better than life, my lips shall praise thee." Psalms 63:3

"O LORD, thou art my God; I will exalt thee, I will praise thy name; for thou hast done wonderful things; thy counsels of old are faithfulness and truth." Isaiah 25:1

"I will praise thee, O Lord my God, with all my heart: and I will glorify thy name for evermore." Psalms 86:12

"To the end that my glory may sing praise to thee, and not be silent. O LORD my God, I will give thanks unto thee for ever."
Psalms 30:12

"Sing unto the LORD, praise ye the LORD: for he hath delivered the soul of the poor from the hand of evildoers." Jeremiah 20:13

"I will sing unto the LORD as long as I live: I will sing praise to my God while I have my being." Psalms 104:33

"I will praise thee, O LORD, with my whole heart; I will shew forth all thy marvellous works. I will be glad and rejoice in thee: I will sing praise to thy name, O thou most High." Psalms 9:1-2

"I will extol thee, my God, O king; and I will bless thy name for ever and ever. Every day will I bless thee; and I will praise thy name for ever and ever. Great is the LORD, and greatly to be praised; and his greatness is unsearchable. One generation shall praise thy works to another, and shall declare thy mighty acts. I will speak of the glorious honour of thy majesty, and of thy wondrous works." Psalms 145:1-5

"So we thy people and sheep of thy pasture will give thee thanks for ever: we will shew forth thy praise to all generations." Psalms 79:13

"Let them praise the name of the LORD: for his name alone is excellent; his glory is above the earth and heaven." Psalms 148:13

"O give thanks unto the LORD; for he is good; for his mercy endureth for ever." 1 Chronicles 16:34

"My mouth shall speak the praise of the LORD: and let all flesh bless his holy name for ever and ever." Psalms 145:21

"And in that day shall ye say, Praise the LORD, call upon his name, declare his doings among the people, make mention that his name is exalted." Isaiah 12:4

"Blessed be the LORD God of Israel from everlasting to everlasting... Praise ye the LORD." Psalms 106:48

"O praise the LORD, all ye nations: praise him, all ye people. For his merciful kindness is great toward us: and the truth of the LORD endureth for ever. Praise ye the LORD." Psalms 117:1-2

"Make a joyful noise unto God, all ye lands: Sing forth the honour of his name: make his praise glorious." Psalms 66:1-2

"Give unto the LORD, O ye mighty, give unto the LORD glory and strength. Give unto the LORD the glory due unto his name; worship the LORD in the beauty of holiness." Psalms 29:1-2

"Let every thing that hath breath praise the LORD. Praise ye the LORD."
Psalms 150:6

"I will greatly praise the LORD with my mouth; yea, I will praise him among the multitude." Psalms 109:30

"And to stand every morning to thank and praise the LORD, and likewise at even(ing)". 1 Chronicles 23:30

"Praise ye him, all his angels: praise ye him, all his hosts. Praise ye him, sun and moon: praise him, all ye stars of light. Praise him, ye heavens of heavens, and ye waters that be above the heavens. Let them praise the name of the LORD: for he commanded, and they were created."
Psalms 148:2-5

God's Word Gives Courage...

"But thou, O LORD, art a shield for me; my glory, and the lifter up of mine head."
Psalms 3:3

"Be of good courage, and he shall strengthen your heart, all ye that hope in the LORD." Psalms 31:24

"When thou liest down, thou shalt not be afraid: yea, thou shalt lie down, and thy sleep shall be sweet." Proverbs 3:24

"Then shalt thou prosper, if thou takest heed to fulfil the statutes and judgments which the LORD charged Moses with concerning Israel: be strong, and of good courage; dread not, nor be dismayed."
1 Chronicles 22:13

"The LORD is my light and my salvation; whom shall I fear? the LORD is the strength of my life; of whom shall I be afraid?"
Psalms 27:1

"In righteousness shalt thou be established: thou shalt be far from oppression; for thou shalt not fear: and from terror; for it shall not come near thee." Isaiah 54:14

"Be strong and of a good courage; be not afraid, neither be thou dismayed: for the LORD thy God is with thee whithersoever thou goest." Joshua 1:9

"Give us help from trouble: for vain is the help of man. Through God we shall do valiantly: for he it is that shall tread down our enemies." Psalms 60:11-12

"Thou drewest near in the day that I called upon thee: thou saidst, Fear not."
Lamentations 3:57

"Hearken unto me, ye that know righteousness, the people in whose heart is my law; fear ye not the reproach of men, neither be ye afraid of their revilings."
Isaiah 51:7

"For I the LORD thy God will hold thy right hand, saying unto thee, Fear not; I will help thee. Fear not... I will help thee, saith the LORD, and thy redeemer, the Holy One of Israel." Isaiah 41:13-14

"I sought the LORD, and he heard me, and delivered me from all my fears."
Psalms 34:4

"... fear not: have not I commanded you? be courageous, and be valiant."
2 Samuel 13:28

"Be not afraid of sudden fear, neither of the desolation of the wicked, when it cometh. For the LORD shall be thy confidence, and shall keep thy foot from being taken." Proverbs 3:25

"But the LORD your God ye shall fear; and he shall deliver you out of the hand of all your enemies." 2 Kings 17:39

"Be strong and of good courage... fear not, nor be dismayed: for the LORD God, even my God, will be with thee; he will not fail thee, nor forsake thee...". 1 Chronicles 28:20

"Wait on the LORD: be of good courage, and he shall strengthen thine heart: wait, I say, on the LORD." Psalms 27:14

"Fear not, O land; be glad and rejoice: for the LORD will do great things." Joel 2:21

God's Word Gives Comfort...

"I will both lay me down in peace, and sleep: for thou, LORD, only makest me dwell in safety." Psalms 4:8

"Sing, O heavens; and be joyful, O earth; and break forth into singing, O mountains: for the LORD hath comforted his people, and will have mercy upon his afflicted." Isaiah 49:13

"And in that day thou shalt say, O LORD, I will praise thee: though thou wast angry with me, thine anger is turned away, and thou comfortedst me." Isaiah 12:1

"Have mercy upon me, O LORD; for I am weak: O LORD, heal me; for my bones are vexed." Psalms 6:2

"And ye shall serve the LORD your God, and he shall bless thy bread, and thy water; and I will take sickness away from the midst of thee." Exodus 23:25

"The LORD is nigh unto them that are of a broken heart; and saveth such as be of a contrite spirit." Psalms 34:18

"For it was neither herb, nor mollifying plaister, that restored them to health: but thy word, O Lord, which healeth all things." Wisdom of Solomon 16:12

"Yea, though I walk through the valley of the shadow of death, I will fear no evil: for thou art with me; thy rod and thy staff they comfort me." Psalms 23:4

"This is my comfort in my affliction: for thy word hath quickened me." Psalms 119:50

"Bless the LORD, O my soul, and forget not all his benefits: Who forgiveth all thine iniquities; who healeth all thy diseases; Who redeemeth thy life from destruction; who crowneth thee with lovingkindness and tender mercies; Who satisfieth thy mouth with good things; so that thy youth is renewed like the eagle's. The LORD executeth righteousness and judgment for all that are oppressed." Psalms 103:2-6

"I have heard thy prayer, I have seen thy tears: behold, I will heal thee...".
2 Kings 20:5

"Heal me, O LORD, and I shall be healed; save me, and I shall be saved: for thou art my praise." Jeremiah 17:14

"For I will restore health unto thee, and I will heal thee of thy wounds, saith the LORD". Jeremiah 30:17

"For thus saith the high and lofty One that inhabiteth eternity, whose name is Holy; I dwell in the high and holy place, with him also that is of a contrite and humble spirit, to revive the spirit of the humble, and to revive the heart of the contrite ones." Isaiah 57:15

"He sent his word, and healed them, and delivered them from their destructions. Oh that men would praise the LORD for his goodness, and for his wonderful works to the children of men!" Psalms 107:20-21

"O LORD my God, I cried unto thee, and thou hast healed me." Psalms 30:2

"Mark the perfect man, and behold the upright: for the end of that man is peace." Psalms 37:37

"I, even I, am he that comforteth you". Isaiah 51:12

"The LORD lift up his countenance upon thee, and give thee peace." Numbers 6:26

"It is of the LORD'S mercies that we are not consumed, because his compassions fail not." Lamentations 3:22

"As one whom his mother comforteth, so will I comfort you". Isaiah 66:13

"Pleasant words are as a honeycomb, sweet to the soul, and health to the bones." Proverbs 16:24

"My presence shall go with thee, and I will give thee rest."   Exodus 33:14

"I create the fruit of the lips; Peace, peace to him that is far off, and to him that is near, saith the LORD; and I will heal him."
Isaiah 57:19

"He healeth the broken in heart, and bindeth up their wounds."   Psalms 147:3

"My defence is of God, which saveth the upright in heart."   Psalms 7:10

"If my people, which are called by my name, shall humble themselves, and pray, and seek my face, and turn from their wicked ways; then will I hear from heaven, and will forgive their sin, and will heal their land."   2 Chronicles 7:14

God's Word Gives Love...

"And thou shalt love the LORD thy God with all thine heart, and with all thy soul, and with all thy might." Deuteronomy 6:5

"Take good heed therefore unto yourselves, that ye love the LORD your God." Joshua 23:11

"Because he hath set his love upon me, therefore will I deliver him: I will set him on high, because he hath known my name. He shall call upon me, and I will answer him: I will be with him in trouble; I will deliver him, and honour him. With long life will I satisfy him, and shew him my salvation." Psalms 91:14-16

"I love them that love me; and those that seek me early shall find me." Proverbs 8:17

"O continue thy lovingkindness unto them that know thee; and thy righteousness to the upright in heart." Psalms 36:10

"And shewing mercy unto thousands of them that love me and keep my commandments." Deuteronomy 5:10

"Look thou upon me, and be merciful unto me, as thou usest to do unto those that love thy name." Psalms 119:132

"Ye that love the LORD, hate evil: he preserveth the souls of his saints; he delivereth them out of the hand of the wicked." Psalms 97:10

"O love the LORD, all ye his saints: for the LORD preserveth the faithful, and plentifully rewardeth the proud doer."
Psalms 31:23

"... what doth the LORD thy God require of thee, but to fear the LORD thy God, to walk in all his ways, and to love him, and to serve the LORD thy God with all thy heart and with all thy soul". Deuteronomy 10:12

"Behold, for peace I had great bitterness: but thou hast in love to my soul delivered it from the pit of corruption: for thou hast cast all my sins behind thy back."
Isaiah 38:17

"Cause me to hear thy lovingkindness in the morning; for in thee do I trust: cause me to know the way wherein I should walk; for I lift up my soul unto thee."
Psalms 143:8

"Thou shalt not avenge, nor bear any grudge against the children of thy people, but thou shalt love thy neighbour as thyself: I am the LORD." Leviticus 19:18

"And he will love thee, and bless thee, and multiply thee: he will also bless the fruit of thy womb...". Deuteronomy 7:13

"Also the sons of the stranger, that join themselves to the LORD, to serve him, and to love the name of the LORD, to be his servants, every one that keepeth the sabbath from polluting it, and taketh hold of my covenant...". Isaiah 56:6

"And it shall come to pass, if ye shall hearken diligently unto my command-ments which I command you this day, to love the LORD your God, and to serve him with all your heart and with all your soul, that I will give you the rain of your land in his due season, the first rain and the latter rain, that thou mayest gather in thy corn, and thy wine, and thine oil. And I will send grass in thy fields for thy cattle, that thou mayest eat and be full."
Deuteronomy 11:13-15

"... for the LORD your God proveth you, to know whether ye love the LORD your God with all your heart and with all your soul."
Deuteronomy 13:3

"The LORD preserveth all them that love him: but all the wicked will he destroy."
Psalms 145:20

"But let him that glorieth glory in this, that he understandeth and knoweth me, that I am the LORD which exercise loving kindness, judgment, and righteousness, in the earth: for in these things I delight, saith the LORD." Jeremiah 9:24

"That thou mayest love the LORD thy God, and that thou mayest obey his voice, and that thou mayest cleave unto him: for he is thy life, and the length of thy days...".
Deuteronomy 30:20

"The way of the wicked is an abomination unto the LORD: but he loveth him that followeth after righteousness."
Proverbs 15:9

"He hath shewed thee, O man, what is good; and what doth the LORD require of thee, but to do justly, and to love mercy, and to walk humbly with thy God?"
Micah 6:8

"Hear me, O LORD; for thy lovingkindness is good: turn unto me according to the multitude of thy tender mercies."
Psalms 69:16

"Know therefore that the LORD thy God, he is God, the faithful God, which keepeth covenant and mercy with them that love him and keep his commandments to a thousand generations". Deuteronomy 7:9

"Withhold not thou thy tender mercies from me, O LORD: let thy lovingkindness and thy truth continually preserve me." Psalms 40:11

"Therefore thou shalt love the LORD thy God, and keep his charge, and his statutes, and his judgments, and his commandments, alway(s)." Deuteronomy 11:1

"But the stranger that dwelleth with you shall be unto you as one born among you, and thou shalt love him as thyself; for ye were strangers in the land of Egypt: I am the LORD your God." Leviticus 19:34

"For whom the LORD loveth he correcteth; even as a father the son in whom he delighteth." Proverbs 3:12

God's Word Gives Strength...

"I will love thee, O LORD, my strength. The LORD is my rock, and my fortress, and my deliverer; my God, my strength, in whom I will trust; my buckler, and the horn of my salvation, and my high tower. I will call upon the LORD, who is worthy to be praised: so shall I be saved from mine enemies." Psalms 18:1-3

"For thou hast been a strength to the poor, a strength to the needy in his distress, a refuge from the storm, a shadow from the heat, when the blast of the terrible ones is as a storm against the wall." Isaiah 25:4

"The LORD will give strength unto his people; the LORD will bless his people with peace." Psalms 29:11

"The LORD is my strength and my shield; my heart trusted in him, and I am helped: therefore my heart greatly rejoiceth; and with my song will I praise him. The LORD is their strength, and he is the saving strength of his anointed." Psalms 28:7-8

"I will go in the strength of the Lord GOD: I will make mention of thy righteousness, even of thine only." Psalms 71:16

"Fear thou not; for I am with thee: be not dismayed; for I am thy God: I will strengthen thee; yea, I will help thee; yea, I will uphold thee with the right hand of my righteousness." Isaiah 41:10

"For the eyes of the LORD run to and fro throughout the whole earth, to shew himself strong in the behalf of them whose heart is perfect toward him."
2 Chronicles 16:9

"He giveth power to the faint; and to them that have no might he increaseth strength. Even the youths shall faint and be weary, and the young men shall utterly fall: But they that wait upon the LORD shall renew their strength; they shall mount up with wings as eagles; they shall run, and not be weary; and they shall walk, and not faint."
Isaiah 40:29-31

"God is our refuge and strength, a very present help in trouble. Therefore will not we fear, though the earth be removed, and though the mountains be carried into the midst of the sea; Though the waters thereof roar and be troubled, though the mountains shake with the swelling thereof." Psalms 46:1-3

"The name of the LORD is a strong tower: the righteous runneth into it, and is safe."
Proverbs 18:10

"But be not thou far from me, O LORD: O my strength, haste thee to help me." Psalms 22:19

"The LORD is my strength and song, and he is become my salvation: he is my God... and I will exalt him." Exodus 15:2

"Unto thee, O my strength, will I sing: for God is my defence, and the God of my mercy." Psalms 59:17

"Or let him take hold of my strength, that he may make peace with me; and he shall make peace with me." Isaiah 27:5

"The way of the LORD is strength to the upright: but destruction shall be to the workers of iniquity." Proverbs 10:29

"Bow down thine ear to me; deliver me speedily: be thou my strong rock, for a house of defence to save me. For thou art my rock and my fortress; therefore for thy name's sake lead me, and guide me. Pull me out of the net that they have laid privily for me: for thou art my strength." Psalms 31:2-4

"Let the words of my mouth, and the meditation of my heart, be acceptable in thy sight, O LORD, my strength, and my redeemer." Psalms 19:14

"Lift up your eyes on high, and behold who hath created these things, that bringeth out their host by number: he calleth them all by names by the greatness of his might, for that he is strong in power; not one faileth." Isaiah 40:26

"Say to them that are of a fearful heart, Be strong, fear not: behold, your God will come with vengeance, even God with a recompence; he will come and save you." Isaiah 35:4

"It is God that girdeth me with strength, and maketh my way perfect." Psalms 18:32

"My flesh and my heart faileth: but God is the strength of my heart, and my portion for ever." Psalms 73:26

"Seek the LORD, and his strength: seek his face evermore." Psalms 105:4

"And I will strengthen them in the LORD; and they shall walk up and down in his name, saith the LORD." Zechariah 10:12

God's Word Gives Truth...

"For the word of the LORD is right; and all his works are done in truth." Psalms 33:4

"For his merciful kindness is great toward us: and the truth of the LORD endureth for ever. Praise ye the LORD." Psalms 117:2

"That he who blesseth himself in the earth shall bless himself in the God of truth; and he that sweareth in the earth shall swear by the God of truth; because the former troubles are forgotten, and because they are hid from mine eyes." Isaiah 65:16

"He shall cover thee with his feathers, and under his wings shalt thou trust: his truth shall be thy shield and buckler." Psalms 91:4

"And thou shalt swear, The LORD liveth, in truth, in judgment, and in righteousness; and the nations shall bless themselves in him, and in him shall they glory."
Jeremiah 4:2

"Only fear the LORD, and serve him in truth with all your heart: for consider how great things he hath done for you."
1 Samuel 12:24

"And the LORD passed by before him, and proclaimed, The LORD, The LORD God, merciful and gracious, longsuffering, and abundant in goodness and truth."
Exodus 34:6

"For he cometh, for he cometh to judge the earth: he shall judge the world with righteousness, and the people with his truth." Psalms 96:13

"For the LORD is good; his mercy is everlasting; and his truth endureth to all generations." Psalms 100:5

"Open ye the gates, that the righteous nation which keepeth the truth may enter in." Isaiah 26:2

"I have chosen the way of truth: thy judgments have I laid before me." Psalms 119:30

"But as for me, my prayer is unto thee, O LORD, in an acceptable time: O God, in the multitude of thy mercy hear me, in the truth of thy salvation." Psalms 69:13

"Justice and judgment are the habitation of thy throne: mercy and truth shall go before thy face." Psalms 89:14

"By mercy and truth iniquity is purged: and by the fear of the LORD men depart from evil." Proverbs 16:6

"But thou, O Lord, art a God full of compassion, and gracious, longsuffering, and plenteous in mercy and truth." Psalms 86:15

"He is the Rock, his work is perfect: for all his ways are judgment: a God of truth and without iniquity, just and right is he." Deuteronomy 32:4

"Behold, thou desirest truth in the inward parts: and in the hidden part thou shalt make me to know wisdom." Psalms 51:6

"Thy righteousness is an everlasting righteousness, and thy law is the truth." Psalms 119:142

"All the paths of the LORD are mercy and truth unto such as keep his covenant and his testimonies." Psalms 25:10

"And they shall be my people, and I will be their God, in truth and in righteousness." Zechariah 8:8

"For my mouth shall speak truth; and wickedness is an abomination to my lips." Proverbs 8:7

"The LORD is righteous in all his ways, and holy in all his works. The LORD is nigh unto all them that call upon him, to all that call upon him in truth." Psalms 145:17-18

"These are the things that ye shall do; Speak ye every man the truth to his neighbour; execute the judgment of truth and peace in your gates". Zechariah 8:16

God's Word Gives Hope...

"But I will hope continually, and will yet praise thee more and more." Psalms 71:14

"Thou art my hiding place and my shield: I hope in thy word." Psalms 119:114

"The LORD is my portion, saith my soul; therefore will I hope in him."
Lamentations 3:24

"Uphold me according unto thy word, that I may live: and let me not be ashamed of my hope." Psalms 119:116

"For in thee, O LORD, do I hope: thou wilt hear, O Lord my God." Psalms 38:15

"It is good that a man should both hope and quietly wait for the salvation of the LORD." Lamentations 3:26

"The LORD taketh pleasure in them that fear him, in those that hope in his mercy." Psalms 147:11

"Happy is he that hath the God of Jacob for his help, whose hope is in the LORD his God: Which made heaven, and earth, the sea, and all that therein is: which keepeth truth for ever: Which executeth judgment for the oppressed: which giveth food to the hungry. The LORD looseth the prisoners: The LORD openeth the eyes of the blind: the LORD raiseth them that are bowed down: the LORD loveth the righteous: The LORD preserveth the strangers; he relieveth the fatherless and widow: but the way of the wicked he turneth upside down." Psalms 146:5-9

"My soul fainteth for thy salvation: but I hope in thy word." Psalms 119:81

"Why art thou cast down, O my soul? and why art thou disquieted within me? hope thou in God: for I shall yet praise him, who is the health of my countenance, and my God." Psalms 42:11

"I have set the LORD always before me: because he is at my right hand, I shall not be moved. Therefore my heart is glad, and my glory rejoiceth: my flesh also shall rest in hope." Psalms 16:8-9

"Be not a terror unto me: thou art my hope in the day of evil." Jeremiah 17:17

"That they might set their hope in God, and not forget the works of God, but keep his commandments". Psalms 78:7

"I wait for the LORD, my soul doth wait, and in his word do I hope." Psalms 130:5

"Blessed is the man that trusteth in the LORD, and whose hope the LORD is."
Jeremiah 17:7

"Behold, the eye of the LORD is upon them that fear him, upon them that hope in his mercy; To deliver their soul from death, and to keep them alive in famine. Our soul waiteth for the LORD: he is our help and our shield. For our heart shall rejoice in him, because we have trusted in his holy name. Let thy mercy, O LORD, be upon us, according as we hope in thee."
Psalms 33:18-22

"For thou art my hope, O Lord GOD: thou art my trust from my youth." Psalms 71:5

"And now, Lord, what wait I for? my hope is in thee." Psalms 39:7

"The hope of the righteous shall be gladness: but the expectation of the wicked shall perish." Proverbs 10:28

"Remember the word unto thy servant, upon which thou hast caused me to hope." Psalms 119:49

"Chasten thy son while there is hope, and let not thy soul spare for his crying." Proverbs 19:18

"And thou shalt be secure, because there is hope; yea, thou shalt dig about thee, and thou shalt take thy rest in safety. Also thou shalt lie down, and none shall make thee afraid". Job 11:18

God's Word Gives Trust...

"Every word of God is pure: he is a shield unto them that put their trust in him."
Proverbs 30:5

"I will say of the LORD, He is my refuge and my fortress: my God; in him will I trust."
Psalms 91:2

"Our soul waiteth for the LORD: he is our help and our shield. For our heart shall rejoice in him, because we have trusted in his holy name."   Psalms 33:20-21

"O my God, I trust in thee: let me not be ashamed, let not mine enemies triumph over me. Bow down thine ear to me; deliver me speedily: be thou my strong rock, for a house of defence to save me."
Psalms 25:1-2

"Who is among you that feareth the LORD, that obeyeth the voice of his servant, that walketh in darkness, and hath no light? let him trust in the name of the LORD, and stay upon his God." Isaiah 50:10

"The LORD redeemeth the soul of his servants: and none of them that trust in him shall be desolate." Psalms 34:22

"Trust in him at all times; ye people, pour out your heart before him: God is a refuge for us." Psalms 62:8

"And he hath put a new song in my mouth, even praise unto our God: many shall see it, and fear, and shall trust in the LORD. Blessed is that man that maketh the LORD his trust, and respecteth not the proud, nor such as turn aside to lies." Psalms 40:3-4

"What time I am afraid, I will trust in thee. In God I will praise his word, in God I have put my trust; I will not fear what flesh can do unto me." Psalms 56:3-4

"Judge me, O LORD; for I have walked in mine integrity: I have trusted also in the LORD; therefore I shall not slide." Psalms 26:1

"How excellent is thy lovingkindness, O God! therefore the children of men put their trust under the shadow of thy wings." Psalms 36:7

"For the LORD God is a sun and shield: the LORD will give grace and glory: no good thing will he withhold from them that walk uprightly. O LORD of hosts, blessed is the man that trusteth in thee." Psalms 84:11-12

"Many sorrows shall be to the wicked: but he that trusteth in the LORD, mercy shall compass him about." Psalms 32:10

"Thou wilt keep him in perfect peace, whose mind is stayed on thee: because he trusteth in thee. Trust ye in the LORD for ever: for in the LORD JEHOVAH is everlasting strength". Isaiah 26:3-4

"Be merciful unto me, O God, be merciful unto me: for my soul trusteth in thee: yea, in the shadow of thy wings will I make my refuge, until these calamities be overpast. I will cry unto God most high; unto God that performeth all things for me. He shall send from heaven, and save me from the reproach of him that would swallow me up. God shall send forth his mercy and his truth." Psalms 57:1-3

"But I trusted in thee, O LORD: I said, Thou art my God." Psalms 31:14

"He shall not be afraid of evil tidings: his heart is fixed, trusting in the LORD." Psalms 112:7

"And they that know thy name will put their trust in thee: for thou, LORD, hast not forsaken them that seek thee." Psalms 9:10

"O LORD my God, in thee do I put my trust: save me from all them that persecute me, and deliver me". Psalms 7:1

"The LORD is good, a strong hold in the day of trouble; and he knoweth them that trust in him." Nahum 1:7

"Commit thy way unto the LORD; trust also in him; and he shall bring it to pass."
Psalms 37:5

"Hold up my goings in thy paths, that my footsteps slip not. I have called upon thee, for thou wilt hear me, O God: incline thine ear unto me, and hear my speech. Shew thy marvellous lovingkindness, O thou that savest by thy right hand them which put their trust in thee from those that rise up against them." Psalms 17:5-7

"Hear my cry, O God; attend unto my prayer. From the end of the earth will I cry unto thee, when my heart is overwhelmed: lead me to the rock that is higher than I. For thou hast been a shelter for me, and a strong tower from the enemy. I will abide in thy tabernacle for ever: I will trust in the covert of thy wings." Psalms 61:1-4

God's Word Gives Understanding...

"So that thou incline thine ear unto wisdom, and apply thine heart to understanding; Yea, if thou criest after knowledge, and liftest up thy voice for understanding; If thou seekest her as silver, and searchest for her as for hid treasures; Then shalt thou understand the fear of the LORD, and find the knowledge of God. For the LORD giveth wisdom: out of his mouth cometh knowledge and understanding." Proverbs 2:2-6

"Let my cry come near before thee, O LORD: give me understanding according to thy word." Psalms 119:169

"The fear of the LORD is the beginning of knowledge: but fools despise wisdom and instruction." Proverbs 1:7

"Great is our Lord, and of great power: his understanding is infinite." Psalms 147:5

"There is no wisdom nor understanding nor counsel against the LORD." Proverbs 21:30

"The fear of the LORD is the beginning of wisdom: a good understanding have all they that do his commandments: his praise endureth for ever." Psalms 111:10

"With him is wisdom and strength, he hath counsel and understanding." Job 12:13

"The fear of the LORD is the beginning of wisdom: and the knowledge of the holy is understanding." Proverbs 9:10

"My mouth shall speak of wisdom; and the meditation of my heart shall be of understanding." Psalms 49:3

"But there is a spirit in man: and the inspiration of the Almighty giveth them understanding." Job 32:8

"The fear of the LORD is the instruction of wisdom; and before honour is humility." Proverbs 15:33

"He hath made the earth by his power, he hath established the world by his wisdom, and hath stretched out the heaven by his understanding." Jeremiah 51:15

"Thy hands have made me and fashioned me: give me understanding, that I may learn thy commandments." Psalms 119:73

"And he hath filled him with the spirit of God, in wisdom, in understanding, and in knowledge, and in all manner of workmanship...". Exodus 35:31

"The entrance of thy words giveth light; it giveth understanding unto the simple."
Psalms 119:130

"Behold, the fear of the Lord, that is wisdom; and to depart from evil is understanding." Job 28:28

"I am thy servant; give me understanding, that I may know thy testimonies."
Psalms 119:125

"The LORD by wisdom hath founded the earth; by understanding hath he established the heavens." Proverbs 3:19

"Therefore hearken unto me, ye men of understanding: far be it from God, that he should do wickedness; and from the Almighty, that he should commit iniquity."
Job 34:10

"For God is the King of all the earth: sing ye praises with understanding." Psalms 47:7

"Blessed be the name of God for ever and ever: for wisdom and might are his: And he changeth the times and the seasons: he removeth kings, and setteth up kings: he giveth wisdom unto the wise, and knowledge to them that know understanding...". Daniel 2:20-21

"Give me understanding, and I shall keep thy law; yea, I shall observe it with my whole heart." Psalms 119:34

"Who hath directed the Spirit of the LORD, or being his counsellor hath taught him? With whom took he counsel, and who instructed him, and taught him in the path of judgment, and taught him knowledge, and shewed to him the way of understanding?" Isaiah 40:13-14

God's Word Gives...

And Keeps on Giving!

Praise God!!

All scripture quoted from the Holy Bible
King James Version.

Arranged by Karen L. Howard

Published 1/12/24 by Amazon

Made in the USA
Columbia, SC
14 December 2024

49375609R00050